Contents

Introduction

This fabulously cool collection of 12 fun and funky cross-stitch projects combines quirky contemporary style with traditional techniques to bring this ancient craft right up to date. A handy practical section explains all the necessary basic skills and materials required, and shows you how to create designs from scratch. Throughout the booklet are small charts with fresh, modern designs that can be used for the actual projects or for anything else you might like to customize.

The projects are wide-ranging, from buttons and badges, to drinks coasters, watch straps and customized clothes. Most make great gifts or stocking fillers, and there are plenty of ideas that are suitable for all the family. All the projects are presented in step-by-step form, with clear photographs for you to follow. We're sure you'll have fun making them.

Buttons

I used to love visiting my grandmother and rummaging through her tin of old buttons. Occasionally I would find a fabric button that looked handmade. Granny explained that she had made them herself, from scraps of my grandfather's old clothes. I loved the idea of being able to make your own buttons from little scraps of fabric, and this project is a great way of using up leftover pieces of aida.

YOU WILL NEED

1 Metal self-cover buttons
2 Scissors
3 Needle
4 Embroidery thread
5 Aida

TIPS

I prefer to use metal self-cover buttons, as I find them a little stronger than plastic and ideal for thicker fabrics such as aida.

It is possible to purchase a self-cover button tool, which helps you connect all the pieces together without your fingers getting sore.

Self-cover buttons are inexpensive and available in all sorts of sizes. Made from metal or plastic, you can buy them online or from your local haberdashery. I have left it to you to decide what design you would like to stitch on your buttons. But do bear in mind that it needs to be small enough to fit on the button you're making.

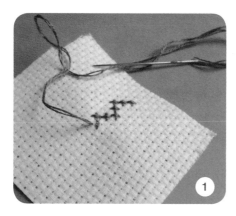

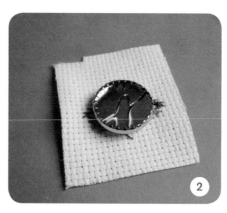

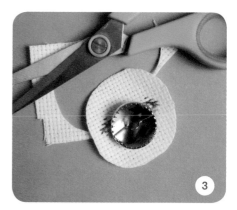

1 Stitch your chosen mini motif to the centre of the scrap of aida.

2 Place the front of the button face down on the reverse of the stitching.

3 Hold the button between your thumb and forefinger and cut around it approximately ½in (1.25cm) from the edge; you will need this extra aida to fold over the edge.

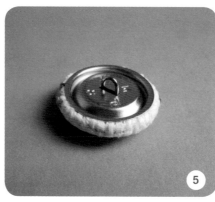

4 Fold the aida over the edge of the button, pressing it firmly into the teeth. You may wish to use the end of the scissors to push it in really tightly.

5 Click the back of the button into place.

6 The button is now complete. Repeat the previous steps and make as many buttons in as many designs as you like.

TIP
Why not update an old cardigan by snipping off its buttons and replacing them with yours? (Just make sure that your buttons fit through the buttonholes first!) Alternatively, use the buttons purely for decoration – stitch them onto a bag or cushion, for instance. The possibilities are endless.

Badges

This is another very simple project that teaches you how to make a felt badge that can be adapted in many other ways. Have fun experimenting by making badges in different shapes and sizes, or make a whole set using complementary designs. If you choose small motifs, you can make a set of badges in no time at all.

YOU WILL NEED

1 Felt
2 Circular bottle top or lid
   to use as a template
3 Aida
4 Needle
5 Scissors
6 Brooch pin
7 Embroidery thread
8 Pencil

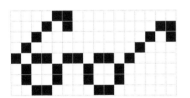

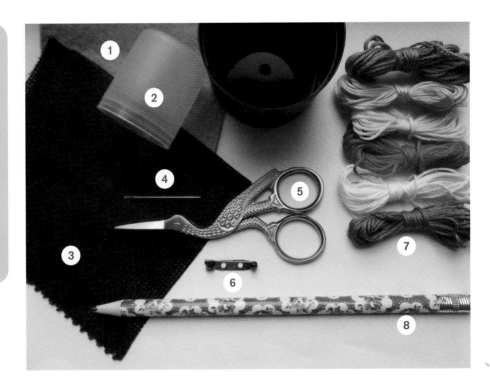

You could add a frill of lace around the edge of the badge to make it into a fancy brooch. Take a strip of lace, pin it between the aida and the felt and use a simple, tiny running stitch (see page 45) to sew it all together.

Alternatively, make a medal. Stitch the badge to the bottom of a short length of ribbon and the brooch pin to the top of the ribbon on the reverse side.

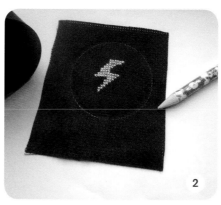

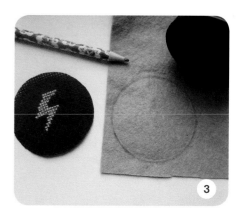

1 Stitch a small motif onto the piece of aida. Choose a bottle top or lid the size you want the badge to be, place it over the stitching and press down gently. Remove the lid: it will have left a circular impression around the design. If the design isn't central, repeat the process until you are satisfied with its appearance.

2 Place the lid back over the impression and draw around it in pencil. Now cut around the pencil marks to leave a little disc of aida with the design in the centre. This will be the front of the badge.

3 To make the back of the badge, place the lid on a colourful piece of felt and draw around it. Cut out this disc and place it beneath the cut-out piece of aida.

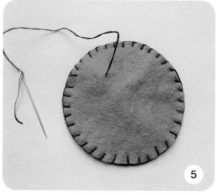

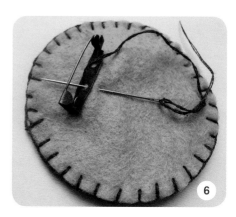

4 Using blanket stitch (see page 46), work your way around the edge of the badge, taking the needle between the layers after the last stitch. The blanket stitching will give the badge a nice edging and should prevent the aida from fraying.

5 Bring the needle out of the back of the badge, either at the centre of the felt backing or towards the top – this will be the position for the brooch pin.

6 The brooch pin will probably have some small holes running along it. Slip the needle through one of these and make a series of little stitches back and forth between the brooch pin and the felt, making sure that the needle only slides through the felt. Repeat until you have stitched all of the holes in the brooch pin to the felt backing. When you have made the last stitch, slide the end of the thread under the felt and brooch pin and pull the needle back up – ideally, at the side of the brooch – and snip off the remaining thread as closely as possible, so that it will never be seen.

Hair Bobbles

If you have mastered the art of making a cross-stitch button (see pages 2–4), you will find making a hair bobble as easy as pie! All the materials required are the same, but with the addition of some thin, colourful hair elastics. The technique is the same, too.

YOU WILL NEED

1 Aida
2 Embroidery thread
3 Thin hair elastics
4 Self-cover buttons
5 Needle
6 Scissors

TIP
Choose a reasonably large button, as anything too small will not show up well in your hair. A good size is ⅞in (2.2cm) or larger.

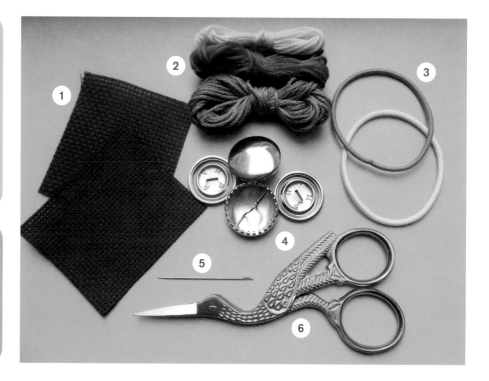

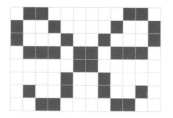

These hair bobbles are fantastic cheap gifts to add to party bags for a child's birthday party or as stocking fillers at Christmas. If you are giving them as gifts, wrap them around a pretty piece of card or a vintage playing card to act as quirky packaging.

There are many things you can do with buttons, so get your thinking cap on and experiment. For example, you could thread a button through your shoe laces for instant jazzed-up pum or thread a piece of ribbon or decorative cord through the back of a button and tie it ar the neck of a bottle of wine as a gift for a friend. Or why not plait some embroidery t add a button and make a friendship bracelet?

TIP
Experiment with different colours − try clashing the colour of the elastic with the colour of the canvas or cross-stitch design.

1 Stitch and assemble the button, following Steps 1−4 of the Buttons project on page 4. You will need one button and one hair elastic per bobble.

2 Push the hair elastic a short way through the shank of the button.

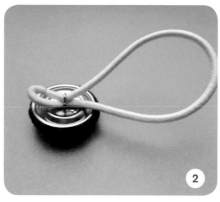

3 Loop one end through the other...

4 ... and pull taut to secure it in place. Hey presto − one completed hair bobble. Repeat to make a matching pair.

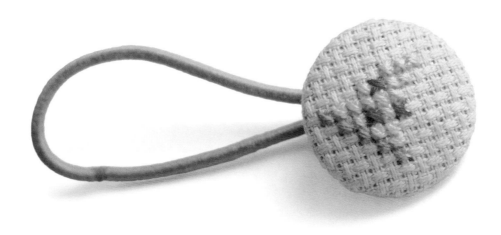

Needle Case

I have been known to leave pins and needles lying around, and they usually end up in someone's foot! I love quirky pincushions, but needle cases are so pretty and are also really easy to make.

YOU WILL NEED

1 Felt in two colours: one piece approximately 7½ x 3½in (19 x 9cm), the other approximately 5 x 2¼in (13 x 6cm)
2 Aida, approximately 2¾ x 2¼in (7 x 6cm)
3 Needle
4 Scissors
5 Embroidery thread
6 Pinking shears

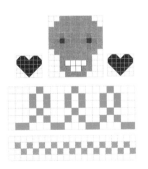

A needle case is like a fabric book, with a single page to keep your pins or needles safe in. There are no set rules for what size or shape a needle case should be. I opted for roughly 3½ x 4in (9 x 10cm) to make it pocket-sized and small enough to carry around in my bag for sewing on the go.

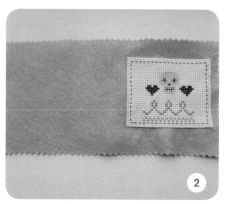

1 Work your design onto the aida. Using pinking shears, snip around the edges of each piece of felt. (This is purely for decorative effect.)

2 The larger piece of felt will be the cover of the needle case. Fold it in half like a book, and attach your completed cross-stitch design to the centre of the front with a simple running stitch (see page 45), using the holes in the aida as a guide to keep the stitches straight and even.

3 Open the cover up. Fold the smaller piece of felt in half and place it in the middle of the cover, aligning the fold with the fold in the cover. This will become the inside page of the needle case.

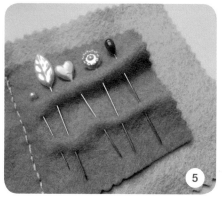

4 With a contrasting colour of thread, attach the inside page to the cover using back stitch or running stitch. Don't worry about the appearance of the stitches too much – just do them as neatly as you can.

5 Gather your pins and needles and stick them into the inside page of the needle case. You will never lose a pin again!

TIPS
Consider adding an extra 'page' of felt into the needle case so that you can store more pins and needles. You could make each one a different colour – but do not add too many pages or the case will become quite bulky.

Make sure the pages are hidden from view when the case is closed by always making the cover page a little bigger in size.

Mini Samplers

Embroidery hoops are usually used to help keep the aida taut while working on it, but they can also double as ready-made frames for your work, with the loop at the top acting as the perfect device to hook onto a nail on a wall. These mini hoops enable you to whip up little pictures in no time at all!

YOU WILL NEED

1 All-purpose glue
2 Felt
3 Aida
4 Embroidery hoops
5 Needle
6 Scissors
7 Pencil
8 Embroidery thread

TIP

You can either stitch the design before adding it to the hoop or work it while it is inside the hoop. I find it easier to stitch without using a hoop, as I can manipulate the fabric more easily and work much faster. If you wish to do the same, simply put the fabric in the hoop after you have completed the stitching, as described in Step 1.

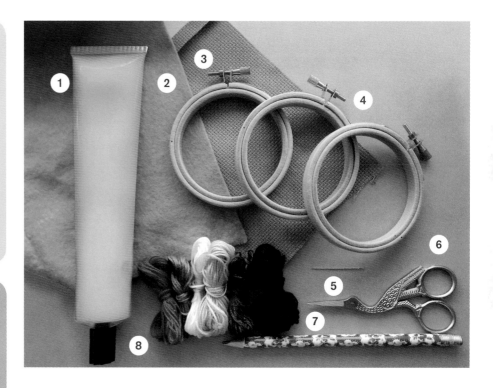

Why not make a set of different-sized samplers, each with a different design, to hang as a collection of themed pictures on your wall? Alternatively, you could stitch a letter onto each hoop so that they spell out a word or message of your choice.

You can add a loop of fancy ribbon or braid to the metal screw at the top of the hoop so that your work can easily be hung, or use this place to tie a decorative bow.

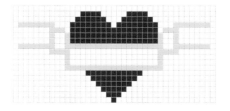

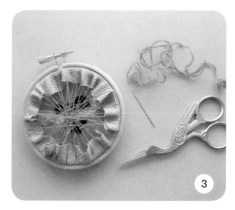

1 Unscrew the embroidery hoop and separate it into two rings. Place the aida over the ring without the screw at the top. This hoop remains at the back of the work. Place the other hoop over the top of the aida, pulling the fabric gently so that it is taut; make sure the aida sits comfortably in the hoop and that the evenweave holes in the fabric are not distorted.

2 When you have set all the stitched motifs into their embroidery hoops, trim off the excess fabric, leaving about 1in (2.5cm) of aida around the edges of the work.

3 Use unwanted embroidery thread or cotton thread to gather all the spare aida at the back of the work. Insert the needle and thread at one side of the hoop, then take it diagonally across to the opposite side, and repeat until all the excess aida has been gathered. You can be as messy as you like here, as this part will not be seen, but it does need to be pulled fairly tight so that it is all held in place securely.

4 Using a pencil, draw around the hoop on a piece of felt. You can use a pen instead of a pencil, of course, but be careful not to mark the wooden hoop with any ink, as it is impossible to remove.

5 Cut out the disc of felt, apply a little glue all around the edge of the gathered fabric, and place the disc of felt on top. Rub away any excess glue and trim any overhanging felt. The mini sampler now has a nice clean backing to it.

6 Repeat steps 1–5 to make as many samplers as you like. Group them to make an attractive wall feature, or make them up as gifts for friends.

Greetings Card

Making your own greetings card is so simple, and the best thing about this project is that it is like a mini work of art: just pop it in a picture frame to mount on the wall and it becomes an instant keepsake. The card and the envelope don't have to be the same colour. Instead, experiment with complementary or clashing colours.

YOU WILL NEED

1 Aperture card with envelope
2 Scissors
3 Embroidery thread
4 Needle
5 All-purpose glue
6 Aida

TIP
Before you do anything, make sure that the area you are working on is as clean as possible, to avoid getting any crumbs or smudges on the card.

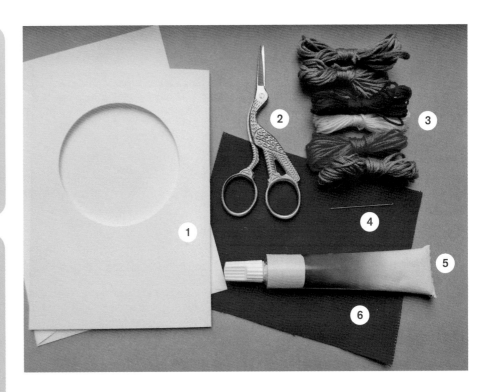

Use a ready-made aperture card: this has a pre-cut frame for your design, with another flap of card that you fold over to cover the messy reverse of the stitching. Aperture cards come in different colours and sizes, and some even have heart-shaped windows. Aperture bookmarks are also available, so you could make a gift for your favourite bookworm.

1 Choose the design you want for your card. What's the occasion? Who's it for? What colours do they like? I chose a bicycle design and stitched it on 14-count aida.

2 Open the card and position the 'window' over the design, making sure it is centred. Cut the aida to approximately 1in (2.5cm) bigger all around than the window.

3 Open the card and squeeze small dots of glue around the edge of the window and the top and bottom edges of the card – but not too close to the edge, as you do not want the glue to ooze out when you close the card.

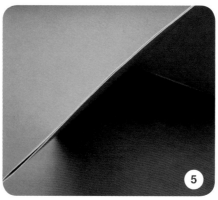

4 Place the piece of aida face down over the window and, while holding it in place, turn the card over to check its position from the front. When you are happy with the placement, smooth the fabric down and press down the left-hand side of the card.

5 Check for any gaps where the card has been glued together. Add a tiny drop of glue using either a brush or a cocktail stick if it is easier, to avoid making a mess. Once all the edges are sealed neatly, your work is done. Leave the card to dry somewhere clean, away from grubby fingertips.

TIP
If the aida looks a little creased when you have finished stitching, you may need to give it a gentle press with an iron before applying it to the card. Use a low heat setting and protect the work by putting a piece of waste fabric over the top (again, make sure it is clean, as it will be making contact with the work). Press the piece gently face down until the creases have disappeared.

Gadget Case

I really like black aida. Well, I like all colours that are a break from boring cream – but I particularly like working on black, as it can make the colours of your floss 'pop'! It is also great for retro computer game designs and never looks too old-fashioned or girly. The trouble is, since it is so dark, it can be almost impossible to see the holes in the fabric, which can make stitching tricky.

YOU WILL NEED

1 Pins
2 Gadget of your choice
3 Embroidery thread
4 Needle
5 Aida
6 Scissors

TIP

When working with black aida, make sure you work in bright natural light or use a daylight bulb in your lamp, and place a piece of white paper or fabric on your lap behind the aida to make it easier to see where the holes are.

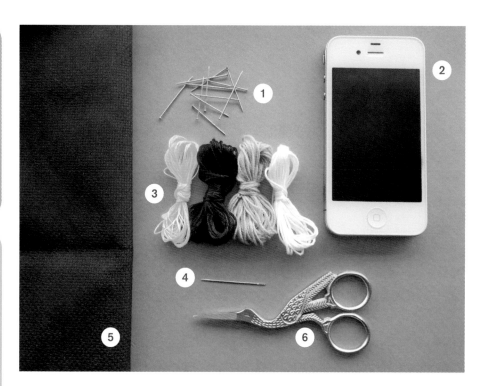

When choosing the design for the gadget case, decide whether you want one that is small enough to sit at the front of the case or one that will cover most of the aida. I chose a retro computer game design as it suited the black aida. It's a good idea to draw around the gadget on a sheet of graph paper, so that you have an idea of how much space you have to work with, and sketch a design in this space. I have not given specific measurements for the aida, as the amount will depend on the size of the gadget. But as a general guide, you will need a piece that can wrap around the gadget about three times its width, with a little spare, and is tall enough to cover the gadget completely.

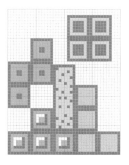

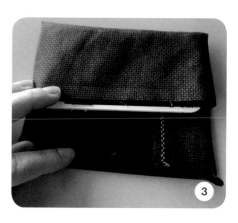

1 Work your chosen design. Place your gadget on the aida, positioning the design where you would like it to sit (I placed mine at the front of my gadget), and fold the fabric around. You want to create a nice cushioned 'blanket' to wrap the gadget in, so you may even want enough aida to have two layers around your gadget.

2 Allow enough aida to fold around the case with a generous overlap, and also plenty at the top and bottom, to fold inside. Make some firm creases as guidelines for where the fabric will fold around the gadget. Cut away any excess aida, using the lines in the evenweave as a guide to cut straight edges.

3 Fold in all the edges so that there are no raw edges at the top, bottom or sides of the case.

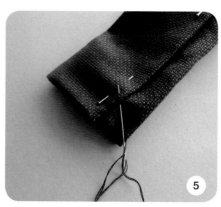

4 Keeping the gadget wrapped in its new blanket, make sure you are happy with the size and fit of the aida. You do not want to wrap the aida so tightly that you cannot remove the gadget easily.

5 Pin the aida in place along the length of the gadget case. Check again that you can slide the gadget in and out easily. Using black embroidery thread or cotton, stitch the seam using small running stitches (see page 45); do not worry too much about what the stitches look like as they will be barely visible. Tuck the end of the thread under the hem and snip off. Remove the pins.

6 Once again, slip the gadget into the aida and pinch together the two layers of aida at the bottom. This will form the base of the case. Stitch along here, just as you did up the side. (You may find it easier to not bother pinning this part, as it is so small. I even kept my gadget inside as I stitched, to help me gauge where it would sit.) Hey presto – one complete gadget case!

Coasters

There are a lot of interesting items on the market that enable you to finish off your cross-stitch projects nicely. As well as picture frames, you can also find plastic drinks coasters, key rings and items such as paperweights to help you transform your humble motif into a ready-made gift.

YOU WILL NEED

1 Aida
2 Plastic drinks coasters
3 Scissors
4 Needle
5 Pencil
6 Embroidery thread
7 Thin cotton fabric for reverse of coaster (optional)

TIP

Instead of using plain fabric for the reverse side of the coaster, you could stitch an identical design on another piece of aida so that it doesn't matter which way up the coaster is placed. Alternatively, why not stitch a different design so you can ring the changes? Just make sure you can fit the two pieces of aida in the coasters when they're shut.

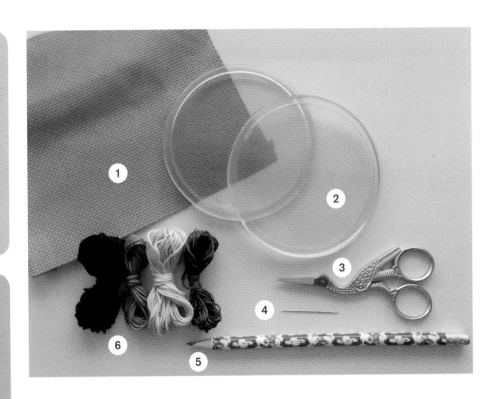

In this project I am going to explain just how simple it is to make a couple of drinks coasters. You could easily create a larger set to keep for yourself or as a house-warming gift for a friend packaged in a nice box.

You will need to buy coasters that are specifically made for craft projects. They will be clear and have a removable back, so that you can place the stitching inside. I found some in my local craft store, but the internet is a good place to search for them.

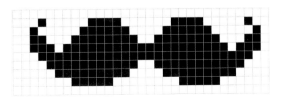

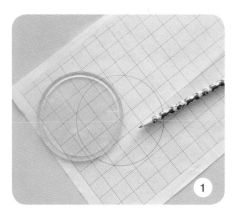

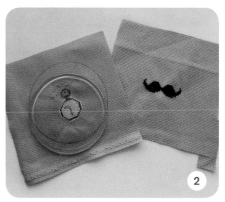

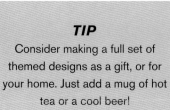

TIP

Consider making a full set of themed designs as a gift, or for your home. Just add a mug of hot tea or a cool beer!

1 Draw around the coaster in pencil on graph paper. This will allow you to gauge what size the design needs to be.

2 Work your design onto the aida. Once complete, place one of the coasters on top, positioning the design in the centre. Draw around the edge in pencil.

3 Cut out the design (**3a**) and place the stitching inside the coaster (**3b**). You may need to trim the edges down to allow it to sit snugly – trim off a tiny piece at a time. If you like, you can cut a piece of thin

cotton fabric the same size as the finished work and insert it in the coaster so that it covers the stitches on the back of the piece. Click the back of the coaster in place and you're finished.

Pop Art Canvases

Binca is a large-scale, evenweave fabric that children use to practise their stitching on, using yarn and a large-eyed needle instead of embroidery thread; the large scale makes it much easier to work on. Projects on binca can be turned around quite quickly. I have demonstrated how to make a bold, Pop Art-inspired set of three canvases with the words Bang, Wham and Pop!

YOU WILL NEED

1 Yarn – can be cheap acrylic

2 Binca

3 Screw-in eyelets

4 Hammer and small tacks or a staple gun

5 Pencil

6 Scissors

7 Three cheap ready-made canvases or wooden frames

8 Large-eyed needle (tapestry needle or a child's plastic needle)

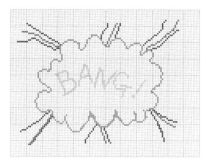

Taking the basic principles of working with binca, you could turn these canvases into many other things. Instead of attaching to the canvas frame, why not cover the binca in stitches to make it a little more robust, stitch a hem around the edge and use it as a lightweight rug? Alternatively, you could make a cushion by doubling the amount of fabric required and filling it with wadding.

1 First of all, get the frames ready. If you have bought cheap, ready-made canvases, as I did, tear off all the canvas.

2 Do not worry too much about removing all the staples – only do so if they are loose or look too messy. Once you have done this, put the frames to one side.

3 Work your pop art designs onto binca, using the yarn in exactly the same way as you would use embroidery thread when cross stitching on aida – but only use one strand of yarn. When the work is complete, place the frame on the back of the stitching and trim off any excess binca, making sure you keep enough to fold over the edges of the frame.

TIPS
While pop art typically uses primary colours, as with all the projects in this booklet, feel free to experiment with colour. You can also buy circular canvases, which may be a fun alternative.

4 Stretch the work over the frame. It may be easier to use a staple gun, but I had tacks to hand so I used those instead. Bring the canvas over the top edge of the frame in the middle of one side and hammer a pin or tack into the wood to hold the fabric in place. Pull the binca over the bottom edge of the frame so that it is taut, and fix another pin or tack in place in the middle of this edge.

5 Working outwards from either side of the central tack, insert tacks along the top and bottom edges of the frame. Check before you insert each one that the binca is taut and not wonky. Tack the sides of the frame in the same way.

6 When you get to the corners, pull the corner of the binca inwards over the frame edge.

7 Fold either side on top of it and tack it in place. This will give a neat, mitred corner.

8 Repeat Steps 1–7 to make the other two canvases. Once all the canvas has been tacked in place, you will need to add some eyelets so that you can hang the work. Turn the work over, so that you are looking at the back. On the upper inside edge of the frame, screw in an eyelet about 1 in (2.5cm) down the side. Place another eyelet on the opposite side of the frame at roughly the same point.

9 Thread a length of yarn through the eyelets and tie in a knot so you can hang the work.

Eye Mask

This fun and colourful eye mask is perfect for keeping out the light and helping you to get a restful night's sleep. I recommend using a brightly coloured aida and embroidery thread with a contrasting ribbon.

YOU WILL NEED

1 Aida, 12 x 8in (30 x 20cm)
2 Felt, 8 x 4in (20 x 10cm)
3 Pen or pencil
4 Embroidery thread
5 Needle
6 Scissors
7 Tracing paper
8 1yd (90cm) ribbon, 1in (2.5cm) wide
9 Pins
10 Sheet of A4 paper

TIP

For a more luxurious eye mask, cut a thin piece of cotton wadding to the same size as the eye mask and sandwich it in between the front and back pieces. Use a soft, satin fabric as the backing fabric, instead of felt.

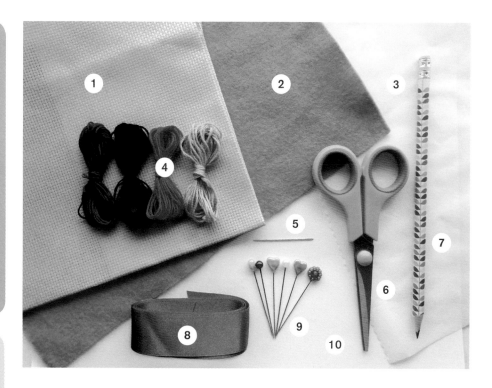

Experiment with different widths of ribbon. A wider ribbon, as pictured, creates a much fuller bow. Choose a very soft, satin ribbon, as it will be more comfortable to sleep in.

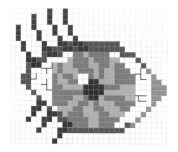

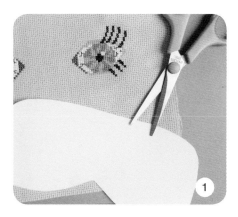

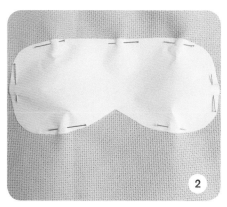

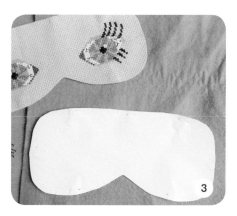

1 Following the chart on page 30, stitch the eyes onto the aida. Trace the template (right) onto a sheet of paper and cut out.

2 Place the paper pattern over the stitched eyes, positioning it so that the eyes are fairly central. Pin the pattern in place.

3 Cut around the edge of the pattern. Remove the pins and pattern. You now have the front of the mask. Pin the pattern to the felt and cut around it; this will form the back of the mask.

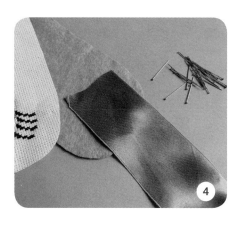

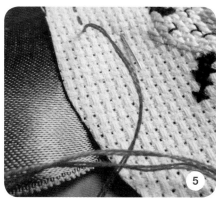

4 Cut the ribbon in half and place one end of each piece on the felt at each side of the mask, with at least 1in (2.5cm) of the ribbon inside the mask to make sure it will be secure. Place the front of the mask on top and pin around the edges to hold the aida, felt and ribbon together.

5 Take a length of embroidery thread and carefully pull away two strands. Thread the needle and work a line of running stitch (see page 45) around the edge of the mask. The aida's evenweave makes it easy to do an evenly spaced running stitch that looks neat on the reverse of the mask, too.

6 To avoid having a knot from the end of the thread on show, take the needle between the felt and aida, pull it through the felt, and cut the end of the thread as close to the felt as possible, leaving the end of the thread sandwiched between the layers and out of sight. The mask is now complete. Sweet dreams!

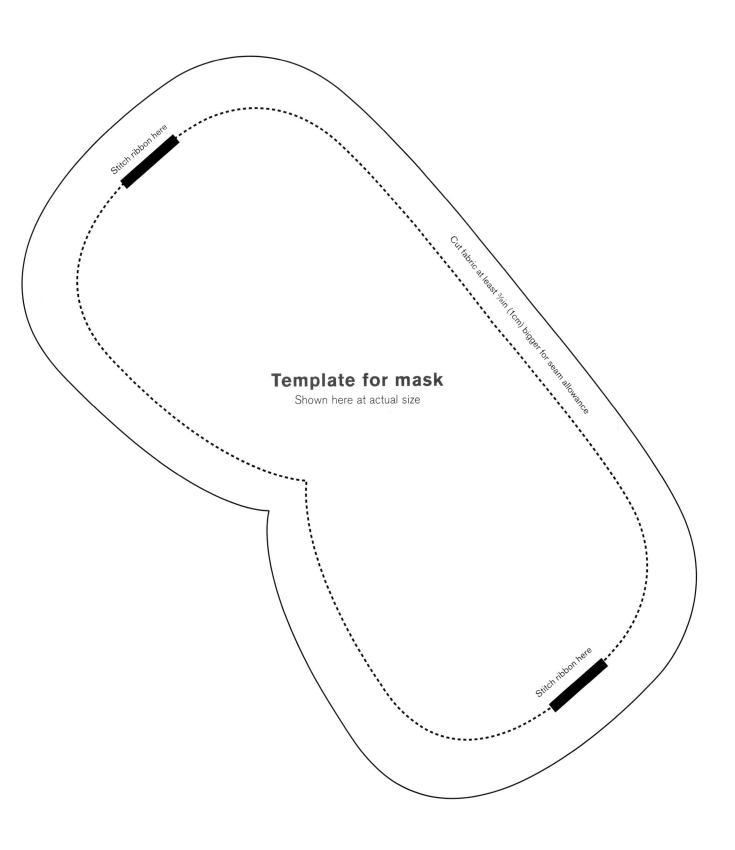

Template for mask

Shown here at actual size

Stitch ribbon here

Stitch ribbon here

Cut fabric at least ⅜in (1cm) bigger for seam allowance

Watch Strap

This is probably one of the most fiddly projects in this book, but I think the results are worth it. I bought the watch face and buckle online. You could just as easily use the parts from an old watch, but the important thing is to find a watch with a bar on either side of the face to attach your aida straps to.

YOU WILL NEED

1 Aida: enough to make 2 strips at least 2½ x 8in (6 x 20cm) – see advice on measurement in Tip below – and a scrap 2½ x 2¾in (6 x 7cm)

2 Watch face with a bar at each side

3 Buckle

4 Embroidery thread

5 Needle

6 Sharp-pointed scissors

TIP

To work out the exact length of aida you'll need, measure the circumference of your wrist, divide by two and add at least ¾in (2cm) to each strip, as you need to allow extra to fold over the watch bars or to add your buckle to later on. For the width, allow approximately three times the width of the watch bars.

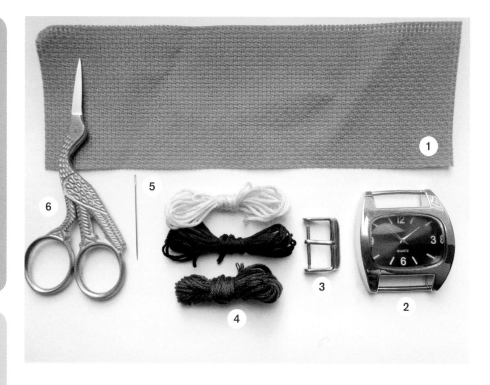

On 14-count aida my design is about ¾in (2cm) wide, which makes it a perfect fit for the watch I chose. Sketch your design of choice on graph paper to see which scale would best fit the width of your bars, and select your aida size accordingly.

It is a good idea to choose a design that has lots of gaps and spaces in it, as you will be making small holes down the centre of the strap for the buckle to sit in. The Navajo-style design I have used is perfect for this, as there are evenly spaced gaps running down the centre of the pattern.

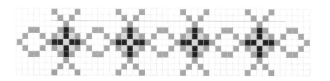

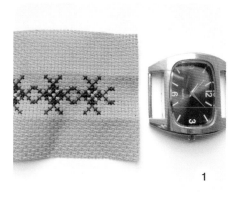

1

2

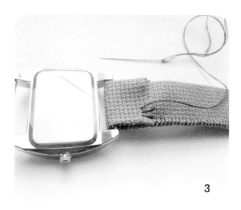

3

1 Take the strips of aida and fold them in half lengthways. Make a crease so that you can find the centre point for the design. Work your chosen design so that it runs approximately 5½in (14cm) down the length of each strip, leaving a little spare aida at each end. Fold each long side of the strip over to the wrong side along the top and bottom edges of the cross stitch, creasing the aida firmly. Check that the folded fabric will fit the watch bars.

2 On the reverse, work little straight stitches down the side, using the holes in the aida as a guide to keep the stitches straight and even in size.

3 Thread one strip through the bottom bar of the watch, fold over about ¾in (2cm) of the unstitched aida, and stitch in place as you did with the seam.

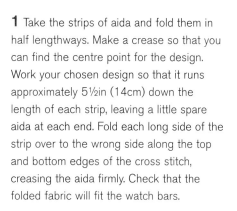

4

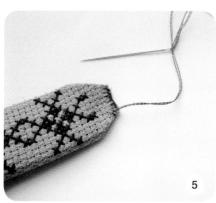

5

6

4 You need to taper the other end of this strap, so that it can slip through the buckle more easily when worn. To do this, poke the sides of the strap inside a little and crease firmly, so that they slope inwards.

5 Stitch in place with small straight stitches to secure.

6 Now make a small band to keep the watch strap in place when worn. Take a strip of aida measuring 2¼ x 2½in (6 x 7cm), fold the long sides in, leaving a strip ¾in (2cm) wide. Stitch up the seam just as you did for the straps.

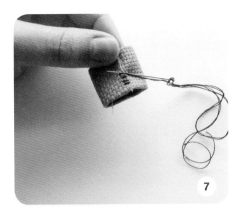

7 Fold the strip around the watch strap and stitch the ends together. Thread this loop onto the remaining strap.

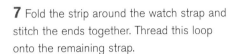

8 Thread one end of the remaining strap through the top bar of the watch and stitch in place, as before. Now decide how long this strap needs to be. I chose to place my buckle about 4in (10cm) down, again leaving ¾in (2cm) at the end to fold over and stitch in place. Slide the buckle onto the end to see where it will sit, and push in the sides of the strap to taper it slightly. With a pair of scissors, push a small hole through the strap and push the tongue of the buckle through it. Fold the end of the strap over the bar of the buckle and stitch it in place.

9 You will need to make some evenly spaced holes down the middle of the strap on the bottom of the watch, where the buckle can sit when worn. Use the tips of your scissors to make these holes, gently pushing through the strap and placing them in the gaps of the design where there are no stitches. There is no need to be too vigorous as you do not want to tear the aida; you just want to make small holes for the tongue of your buckle to fit through.

TIP
The bars at either side of my watch face were about ¾in (2cm) wide – anything less and the cross-stitch design would have to be very small. The wider it is, the more space and freedom you have to create your design.

Customized Shirt

This project shows how to use cross stitch to revamp items of clothing. I chose a lacy design to update an old denim shirt. I decided it would look good running along the straight line of the seam on the shoulders, and chose a deep berry-red shade of thread for a subtle effect.

YOU WILL NEED

1 Item of clothing to customize
2 Embroidery thread
3 Water-soluble canvas
4 Needle
5 Pins
6 Scissors
7 Bowl for hot, soapy water
8 Clean cloth or sponge

TIP

Check the care instructions on the clothing first, as you will have to hand wash the area of stitching in hot, soapy water. If the colours are likely to run because it is new, or if the fabric might shrink, wash and dry it before you work the cross-stitch motif. Use the kind of mild soap you would use to wash dishes with – avoid strong detergents.

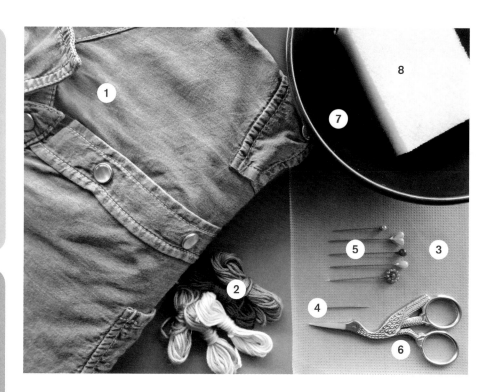

Preparation is key for this project. First you need to decide on the design and where you want it to go on the item of clothing. It's then a good idea to draw the design onto a piece of graph paper to the same scale as your water-soluble canvas. This will give you an idea of how big the design will be when stitched, and whether it will fit into the chosen area on your clothing. It may take a few attempts, especially if you're attempting quite an ambitious design, but persevere, because the end result will be worth it: a one-off item of clothing!

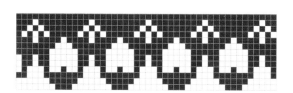

1 Cut a piece of water-soluble canvas big enough to cover the area you will be working on and pin it in place (1a). Once you are happy with the positioning, use some spare embroidery thread or cotton to tack it in place, then remove the pins (1b); the stitches do need not be neat, as they will be removed when you have finished.

2 Now work the cross-stitch motif on the water-soluble canvas in the same way that you would on aida. It is impossible for the motif to sit perfectly flat and taut against the material, but the stitches will still look neat. When you have completed the design, unpick the tacking stitches (2a) and trim off any excess water-soluble canvas (2b).

3 Fill a bowl with hot, soapy water. Dunk the cross-stitched area into the bowl and rub over the stitches gently with your hands. You can also use a clean cloth or sponge, but do not rub hard as you don't want to damage the stitching. The canvas will start to feel soft and rubbery and after 5–10 minutes it will have disappeared. Rinse with clean water and leave to dry.

Tools & Materials

One of the joys of cross stitch is that you need relatively little in the way of specialist tools and materials. This section introduces you to all the basic fabrics, threads and equipment.

AIDA

Aida is the name of the fabric used for cross-stitch and needlepoint projects. It is an 'evenweave' fabric. This means that, when you look closely, it is woven to reveal evenly spaced holes – so each stitch is the same size and shape and the finished work looks very neat, with minimal effort on your part. Each square on the aida represents where one 'x' or cross stitch will go.

Aida comes in various sizes, and each size will alter the size of the finished work. Each size is named as a 'count'. You can get sizes such as '14-count' or '18-count' and this relates to how many little holes there are per inch (2.5cm); for example, 14-count aida has 14 little holes per inch. The higher the count and the more holes per inch, the smaller the finished cross-stitch motif will be as you have a greater number of stitches to fit in. I usually work with 14-count aida, but if I want a piece to finish a little smaller I opt for 18-count to scale it down slightly. Get a scrap of each count of aida and try stitching the same motif on each to compare the finished size.

Do not slip into the habit of buying aida in cream or white all the time – there are many colours available now that can make your work look so much better. There are even aidas available with pre-printed polka-dot patterns on them, and aida that has metallic thread running through it.

BINCA

Binca is like aida on a large scale. It is often used by children to help them learn to sew, as the holes are much bigger and easier for them to see. It can be fun to use for large-scale projects. If you'd like to give it a go, I used it for the Pop Art Canvases on pages 26–29.

WATER-SOLUBLE CANVAS

This is one of my new favourite things. Pin or tack it to ordinary fabric and work your cross stitches in exactly the same way as you would with aida. Then wash the piece in hot, soapy water – the canvas will disappear, leaving behind your neatly worked stitches. It allows you a little creative freedom from working on aida all of the time.

EMBROIDERY THREAD

There are a few very well-known brands of embroidery thread on the market. I do not buy for the brand alone: I choose the shade I am looking for at the time. I also have a lot of embroidery thread that is very cheap and I do not want to discourage you from doing the same. However, there is, of course, a difference in quality and you may find that cheaper threads are more prone to snagging and snapping midway through your stitching. I have even acquired a lot of threads second hand, which is great, but it can be frustrating if you run out of a shade and can't find a matching one again. If you buy your thread new, it will come with a shade number on the label; try to keep hold of this if you like the colour.

As with the aida, there are many exciting varieties of thread available now, from neon to metallic. I love metallic thread, although it can be a little frustrating to work with, as it snags and tangles a lot. I find it easier if I keep my thread much shorter than I would normally and ensure that the thread on each stitch is pulled a little tighter.

NEEDLES

As unprofessional as it may sound, I do not buy any fancy needles. I tend to use whatever I can get my hands on at the time. Ideally, though, I don't like using a needle that is too sharp and I like the 'eye' to be a good size for easy threading, and not so big that it will distort any of the holes in the aida as you thread it though.

PINS

All sewing boxes should have a stash of pins. You never know when you may need them, and you will certainly require them for some of the projects in this book. Add a novelty pin cushion to the mix.

EMBROIDERY HOOPS

Hoops are typically used to hold the aida taut while you work, but they can also act as a decorative frame to complete the project. I prefer to stitch without a frame because I find I can work a lot faster.

GRAPH PAPER AND COLOURED PENCILS

If you wish to design your own cross-stitch charts, you will need to get hold of some graph paper. Use coloured pencils to draw your designs onto the grid. You could buy a graph-paper sketchbook: carry one in your bag and sketch ideas on the go.

BITS AND BOBS
Apart from fabric and threads, there are many other sewing accessories that will come in very handy. Keep a look out for eye-catching vintage or novelty accessories to perk up your sewing box.

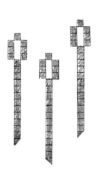
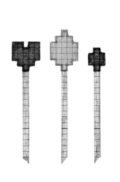
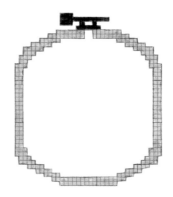
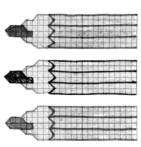

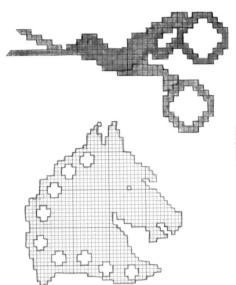

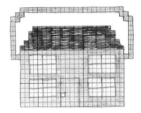

SCISSORS

I use a small pair of scissors for snipping my threads. Bird-shaped scissors like the ones I use are not essential, of course! I also have a large pair of scissors for cutting fabric, and a pair of pinking shears for creating a zigzag edge to reduce fraying or just for decorative purposes. If you're planning to make paper patterns, keep a pair of scissors just for cutting paper; if you use your best fabric scissors for this, they'll blunt really quickly.

THREAD HOLDERS

If you like to keep things organized, you can purchase various things to wrap your thread around to keep it tidy and prevent it from becoming tangled. I have a plastic horse-head tidy, which has several holes dotted around the edge that allow me to thread my thread through and keep it neat. You can also get things such as little cards to wrap your thread around, or perhaps you could even make your own.

TAPE MEASURE AND RULER

These are essentials in any sewing kit, as you will need to take measurements for sewing projects or use a tape measure to work out how large a design will be when finished. A ruler will come in very handy when working your designs onto graph paper, to help you find the centre point.

THIMBLE

A thimble may sound somewhat old fashioned, but let me warn you – cross stitch is a dangerous game! I do not use a thimble, but as a result I am covered in scratches and have a little hole mark in my ring finger from where I repeatedly push my needle onto it. I have also been known to get so close to my work that I scratch my face with my needle. Try not to be as foolish as me!

SEWING BOX

You will need a box to keep all of this equipment in. For a long time I had all of my threads shoved into an old shoe box, but I am now the proud owner of a novelty house-shaped sewing box. I love it to bits and it is huge so I can easily fit everything I need in there.

How to Cross Stitch

While all the projects in this book are based on cross stitch, there are a few other stitches that you will need to learn.

When it comes to embroidery, I am sure everyone has their own techniques and methods, even when it comes to the silliest little details. I am going to explain my own way of working, but if you have been told another way, or are happier doing things in a style you already feel confident in, then please continue to do so.

STARTING OFF

Grab a skein of embroidery thread. Find the loose end of thread, pull until you have about a forearm's length of thread free and snip it off. If you look closely, you will see that the thread is made up of six tiny strands. I like to use two strands in my work, but some people prefer to use three. This is all personal preference. I would suggest using two for the time being, or experimenting with both on a scrap of aida.

Carefully pull two (or three) strands of thread away and thread your needle. At the other end, you're faced with an option: to knot or not to knot the end of your thread. For a long time, I was perfectly happy putting a tiny knot at the end of my thread, until I realized that many other people don't bother; now I rarely knot the end of my thread. If you put a knot in, you run a tiny risk of it creating a bit of a 'bump' in your finished piece.

As an alternative to making a knot, I just leave the end of my thread loose. As I make my first stitch, I leave about

¾in (2cm) of thread loose at the back of the work. As I stitch, this usually gets caught up with my other stitches.

CROSS STITCH

I hate to point out the obvious, but 'cross stitch' is exactly that – stitches that resemble a little 'x' shape. Each stitch is worked in two parts – first, a diagonal stitch in one direction, then another worked on top of it in the opposite direction. On aida evenweave fabric, you bring your needle up through one of the tiny holes, then bring it across the 'square' in the fabric, and diagonally down into the next hole. I like to work from top right, down to the bottom left hole, but it doesn't matter which way you wish to work, so long as

every stitch looks the same, with every stitch on the bottom and every stitch on the top running at the same angle. This will make the finished piece look neat.

HALF CROSS STITCH

This stitch is just half of one completed cross stitch (see illustration, below). When working large areas of the same colour, it can be a good idea to work all of the first diagonal 'half stitches' first, before returning to complete the 'x' stitch. Some people like to work all of their cross stitch in this way, by filling most of their work with half stitches and then completing it. It can make you feel as if you are completing your work a little faster!

Cross stitch

Half cross stitch

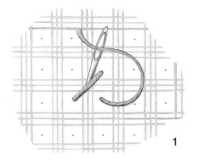

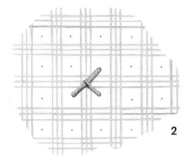

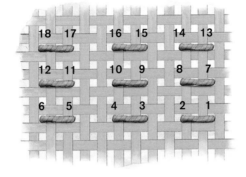

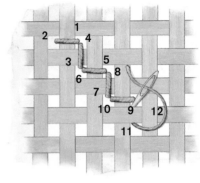

THREE-QUARTER STITCH

When you are reading a cross-stitch chart and encounter a square that is only half coloured in and resembles a triangle, you do not need to complete a full cross stitch. Make the first half of the cross stitch and bring the needle up through the aida to begin the final stitch – but instead of pushing it down into the opposite hole, push it through the middle of the square in the canvas, so that you are just skimming past the middle of the first stitch (**1**). The stitch will now only take up half of the square in the aida, just like the triangle on the chart (**2**).

RUNNING STITCH

This stitch is as easy as pie and is probably the simplest stitch around. Simply bring the needle up through the fabric and then, leaving a slight space, take it back down again to form a straight line. All the stitches should be of equal length if you want your work to look well finished, and each stitch is straight. You could play around with grouping the stitches together to form a block of colour (as above) or experiment with different lengths of stitches.

BACKSTITCH

Backstitch is very similar to running stitch. Instead of running all of your stitches forward and leaving a space between each one, once you have completed one stitch, imagine where the next stitch would be; bring the needle up at the end of this imaginary stitch, then take it back down next to where the last stitch ended. You should have two stitches sitting right next to each other, either in a straight line or at angles (as shown above).

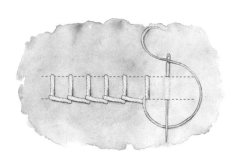

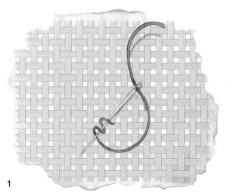

1

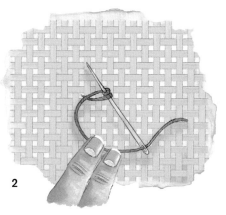

2

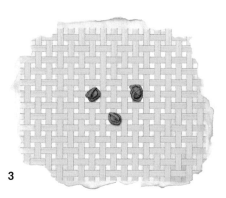

3

BLANKET STITCH

Give your finished work a pretty edge with blanket stitch. Bring the needle up through the aida at the edge of the work. Leaving a slight space as you would when working a running stitch (see page 45), push the needle back down through the aida, but instead of pulling the thread through tightly, leave a little loop. Bring the needle back up through this loop and pull gently. Repeat by bringing the needle through the aida from the back of the work to the front, leaving an equal space again, and threading the needle through the loop of thread at the top again. You should now have a series of straight stitches parallel to each other, with a piece of thread along the bottom linking them together.

FRENCH KNOT

A lot of cross-stitch charts use French knots to act as 'eyes' on characters and motifs. You need to use both hands when completing this stitch, so it can be a bit fiddly. Bring the needle up through the work in the spot you would like the French knot to be placed. Wrap the thread around the needle once or twice (**1**), then push the needle back through the canvas in roughly the same hole that you brought it up through. While doing so, make sure the threads are pulled taut (**2**) so that the knot you create is as neat as possible (**3**).

FINISHING OFF

When I have finished a piece of work, I simply pass my needle and thread through the back of a few stitches and snip it off. If you make a knot, it can be messy and create a bumpy finished piece, especially if you are using a lot of different colours in a small space. By passing the thread through the back of a few stitches on the reverse of the work, you will keep that little piece of thread neatly held in place. If you just cut the thread at the back, you run the risk of stitches coming loose.

With small pieces of work, you probably won't see any creases in the aida, but for larger-scale work it is always a good idea to give it a gentle press under an iron. To be on the safe side, place a piece of clean thin fabric or a sheet of greaseproof paper over the work to protect it from the iron just in case it is dirty.

Understanding charts

To put it very simply, cross-stitch charts look like a big grid. Each square on that grid stands for a single cross stitch.

GET CREATIVE

You do not have to use the designs exactly as they appear in this book. Many of the designs can be broken down into smaller motifs that you could use on their own.

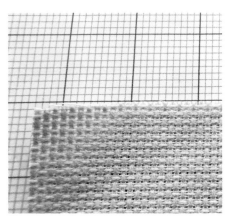

Graph paper and 10-count aida fabric

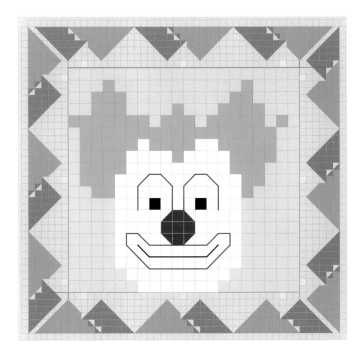

Cross-stitch charts can consist of either black-and-white symbols on a grid, with each symbol relating to a different-coloured thread, or they can be coloured squares on a grid. The latter style of chart is a much easier to follow, as you don't have to keep referring to a key to work out which symbol relates to which colour.

The size of squares on the graph paper should correspond with the size of squares on the aida. Each square of aida fabric has a hole at each corner. Work a cross stitch so that it covers each of these squares.

Throughout the booklet are charts with motifs. Feel free to copy these to use in the projects or to create entirely different designs. However, if you are new to cross stitch, I recommend you choose a small motif and practise it on a scrap of aida first. I tend to work with whichever threads are lurking in my sewing box, so you could do the same. If, however, you're shopping for threads to use with these charts, you could always take this booklet with you, so that you can compare the chart colours with the shades of embroidery thread available.

Designing cross stitch

For me, this is the best bit. As much as I enjoy the actual stitching of the work, I really enjoy coming up with designs and I hope that you will, too.

Cross-stitch designs can be done in a number of ways, but the most popular method is to use graph paper. Since each square represents a single cross stitch, you can colour in the graph paper with your chosen design and work from that. Use graph paper that is exactly the same size as the aida you will be using – which means that the size of your design on the paper will be exactly the same size as on your aida! This has been a real help for me when making my own work. Here are the stages I go through when designing a cross-stitch motif.

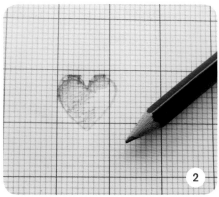

Each square represents one stitch

1 To use the graph paper, you could just dive straight in and colour the individual blocks, but sometimes I find it easier to sketch the design really roughly onto the paper, as here.

2 I then try to make the sketch fit the grid better by drawing over the rough lines and following the squares on the paper.

3 Once I have a rough sketch, I copy it out again so that I can see it more clearly. Then I can have fun playing with colour. If you want the image to have a smoother outline, use three-quarter stitches to form a little 'triangle' instead of a full cross stitch. These help to add shape to the work.

GET INSPIRED

You can use graph paper to copy out some of the charts and alter them by changing the colours or by adding or removing some of the stitches. You can also use graph paper to draw around a frame or object that you would like your work to sit in, to get an idea of how much space you have to stitch your work in. This may seem really basic, but why overcomplicate things?